Welcome to England

By Elma Schemenauer

The
Child's
World®

Published by The Child's World®
1980 Lookout Drive
Mankato, MN 56003-1705
800-599-READ
www.childsworld.com

Content Adviser: Professor Eliga H. Gould, Department of History,
University of New Hampshire, Durham, NH
Design and Production: The Creative Spark, San Juan Capistrano, CA
Editorial: Emily J. Dolbear, Brookline, MA
Photo Research: Deborah Goodsite, Califon, NJ

Cover and title page photo: Geoff du Feu/Alamy
Interior photos: Alamy: 18 (Francisco Martinez); AP Photo: 30 (Sang Tan); Corbis: 9 (Kit
Houghton), 12 (Corbis), 23 (Paul Seheult; Eye Ubiquitous), 24 (Anthony West); Getty Images:
10 (Amanda Hall/Robert Harding World Imagery), 20 (DreamPictures), 25 (Clive Rose), 26–27
(Carl de Souza/AFP); iStockphoto.com: 3 bottom, 6 (Peter Guess), 7 (Steve Irwin), 13 (Karl
Dolenc), 28 (Ross Lewis), 29 (Yoko Bates), 31 (Steve Geer); Panos Pictures: 3 top, 14 (J.C.
Tordai), 16 (David Rose), 19 (Heidi Bradner), 21 (Karen Robinson); Photolibrary Group:
3 middle, 8, 11, 17.
Map: XNR Productions: 5

Library of Congress Cataloging-in-Publication Data
Schemenauer, Elma.
  Welcome to England / by Elma Schemenauer.
      p. cm. — (Welcome to the world)
  Includes index.
  ISBN 978-1-59296-970-8 (library bound : alk. paper)
  1. England—Juvenile literature. 2. England—Social life and customs—Juvenile literature.
I. Title. II. Series.

  DA27.5.S345 2008
  942—dc22
                                                        2007034770

Contents

Where Is England?

What if you were in a spacecraft high above Earth? You would see huge land areas with water around them. These land areas are called **continents.**

Although England is on an island, it is part of the continent of Europe. A narrow strip of water called the English Channel separates England from France. Waters around England include the Irish Sea and the North Sea.

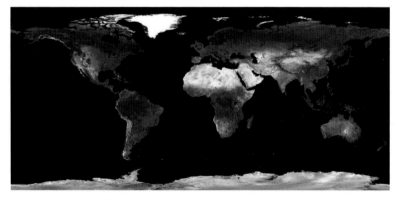

This picture gives us a flat look at Earth. England is inside the red circle.

4

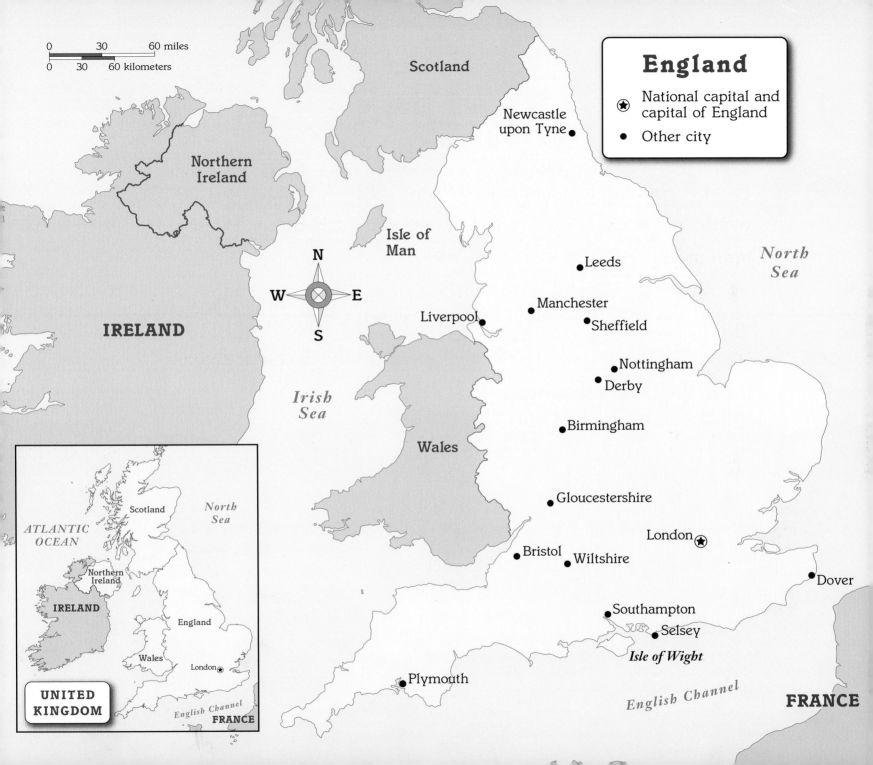

The Land

England is shaped like a tall, knobby triangle. In the north are rugged uplands and mountains. In the middle and southeast are low-lying lands and gentle hills. Most of England's big cities are here.

In the southwest are rugged uplands and **moors.** They are lonely, open grasslands. In the southwest are low

Loweswater is one of numerous lakes in northwestern England's beautiful Lake District.

The southeastern town and seaport of Dover, England, is famous for its white chalk cliffs.

plateaus with **highlands** rising above them. Several highlands are made of granite. Near the coast, the plateaus end in cliffs. There are also cliffs on the southeastern coast—the famous white cliffs of Dover.

Plants and Animals

Elms, oaks, and beeches once covered much of England. People cleared many trees for farming, but some forests still exist. They include newly planted pines and spruces. Grasses and low shrubs such as heather grow on England's windswept moors.

Wild ponies trot over the moors. Among England's other wild animals are hedgehogs, weasels, deer, and red foxes. Otters play in some of the rivers, and seals swim along the seacoasts. Fish include sole, haddock, and herring. Among the country's many birds are swans, wrens, pipits, and blackbirds.

A hedgehog in grass

A small group of wild ponies graze on the moors of Exmoor.

Long Ago

Hunters, farmers, stoneworkers, and tin miners were among early people in what is now England. About 2,600 years ago, iron-working Celts (KELTS) from northern Europe settled there. Road-building Romans took over a few hundred years

After he became king of England, William I began building the Tower of London.

later. Then came German-speaking Angles and Saxons, followed by seagoing Vikings.

The last to invade England were French-speaking Normans. A Norman ruler named William I became king of England in the year 1066.

Many kings and queens followed William I. In the 1500s, during Queen Elizabeth I's rule, the English settled Newfoundland in Canada. They also tried to start a **colony** on Roanoke Island in what is now North Carolina.

The Bayeux Tapestry is a heavy cloth woven with colorful scenes of William I's victory in 1066.

From then on, the English roamed the seas, starting colonies around the world. As this great empire spread, so did its language and ideas about fairness in government. After 1707, when England, Scotland, and Wales joined to form Great Britain, this empire became the **British Empire.**

England Today

Elizabeth II is queen of the United Kingdom.

Today, England is the most powerful part of the United Kingdom. Over time, ties with its former colonies have loosened. Independence for some came after struggle and bloodshed. But most former colonies are now friendly with the United Kingdom. The country works closely and trades with the rest of Europe.

Unlike many countries, England still has a **monarch**— Queen Elizabeth II. She lives in a palace, meets with the prime minister, and hosts world leaders. But the true government leader is the prime minister, who is elected by the people.

This London skyline near the River Thames includes the London Eye—one of the world's largest Ferris wheels.

Festival Pier

English people have many different cultural, racial, and religious backgrounds.

The People

A few people in England, especially in the county of Cornwall, have mainly Celtic backgrounds. But most people in England are English. They have mixed backgrounds. Their family histories include the Celts, Romans, Angles, Saxons, Vikings, and Normans who arrived long ago.

Since the 1950s, many people from former British Empire colonies have moved to England. They include people from India, Pakistan, the West Indies, Guyana, Australia, and Africa. Some Southeast Asians, Chinese, Americans, and other Europeans also live in England. Many of these people live in England's cities.

City Life and Country Life

Most English people live in cities or towns. For some, home is an apartment called a flat. Others live in small two-story houses with little gardens. Houses are often built of brick, stone, or cement blocks. When city people go shopping, they often see beautiful old shops, banks, churches, and museums as well as modern buildings.

In the country, most people live in cottages or houses. These are often in small villages called hamlets.

Did you know?

The London subway system is called the Underground. Some red doubledecker buses still run their routes in London.

16

This house in the English seaside village of Selsey has a thatched, or straw, roof.

Schools and Language

All English children between the ages of five and 16 must go to school. Most students attend local state schools run by the government. Some children pay to attend independent schools. Unlike in the United States, these schools are called public schools!

England's official language is English. It is based on the German spoken by the Angles and Saxons, and the French

A class stands with its teacher at this East London school. Here students from 27 different countries speak more than 30 languages!

spoken by the Normans long ago. But words from many other languages, including Celtic, Latin, and Norwegian, are also part of the English language. English has changed a lot over time, and it keeps on changing.

Workers at the Rolls Royce plant in Derby build an aircraft engine.

Work

In the past, coal powered many English factories. Today, many run on oil or natural gas. English factory workers make such things as cars, airplanes, teapots, woolen mittens, and computer software.

A farmer feeds pigs at her organic farm in Wiltshire.

Many English people have service jobs. They work in hotels, tourist offices, banks, shops, museums, and insurance companies. They serve people from England as well as visitors from around the world.

In the country, some English people farm. They raise sheep, cattle, hogs, barley, vegetables, wheat, and potatoes. Some mine coal, stone for building, or clay for making dishes. Others extract oil and natural gas from deep underground.

Food

Many English dishes use local foods. Lamb from English farms is used in a delicious stew called Lancashire hot pot. Milk from English cows makes cheeses such as cheddar and Stilton. Seacoast fish and farm potatoes make fried fish and chips, a favorite takeout meal. English farmers have started growing sugar beets, too. Their sweetness flavors English desserts such as trifle.

People from other lands have also brought their foods to England. There are restaurants serving everything from American hamburgers to Indian curries to Japanese sushi.

Did you know?

An English pub is a social club, bar, and restaurant, all in one. In the past when travelers rode horses, pubs even had stables! Today pubs serve filling meals that don't cost very much.

A mother and daughter eat battered fish and chips wrapped in paper.

HOURS OF
OPENING

SUN 12.00 - 10.00
MON 11.30 - 11.00
TUES 11.30 - 11.00
WED 11.30 - 11.00
THURS 11.30 - 11.00
FRI 11.30 - 11.00
SAT 11.30 - 10.00

FISH
AND
CHIPS

TO EAT HERE
OR TAKE AWAY

MON-FRI
11.30-11.30 AM

SAT-SUN
11.30-10.00 AM

Hiking is a popular pastime in England. These hikers in the Lake District have stopped to read a map.

Pastimes

English people enjoy staying at home, gardening, fixing up their houses, playing video games, reading, and watching TV. English TV shows are often so good that they find their way to other lands, including the United States.

Riding horses, bicycling, walking in the country, and bird-watching are other popular activities. Some people keep a lifelong list of birds they have seen. England's favorite sports are cricket, soccer, rugby, lawn bowling, golf, and tennis.

Young cricketers play at a club in London.

Holidays

Bank holidays are official holidays for everyone in England. Christmas, Boxing Day, New Year's, and May Day are some of the bank holidays. Boxing Day is the first weekday after Christmas. On this day the English give Christmas boxes or gifts to letter carriers and other service workers.

Special events often take place on bank holidays. One is the cheese race in the county of Gloucestershire. A huge round cheese is rolled down a hill and people chase it. Whoever catches the cheese gets to keep it.

There are many interesting things to see and do in England. Maybe someday you'll visit this beautiful country full of history.